What D[illegible]?

by Wiley Blevins

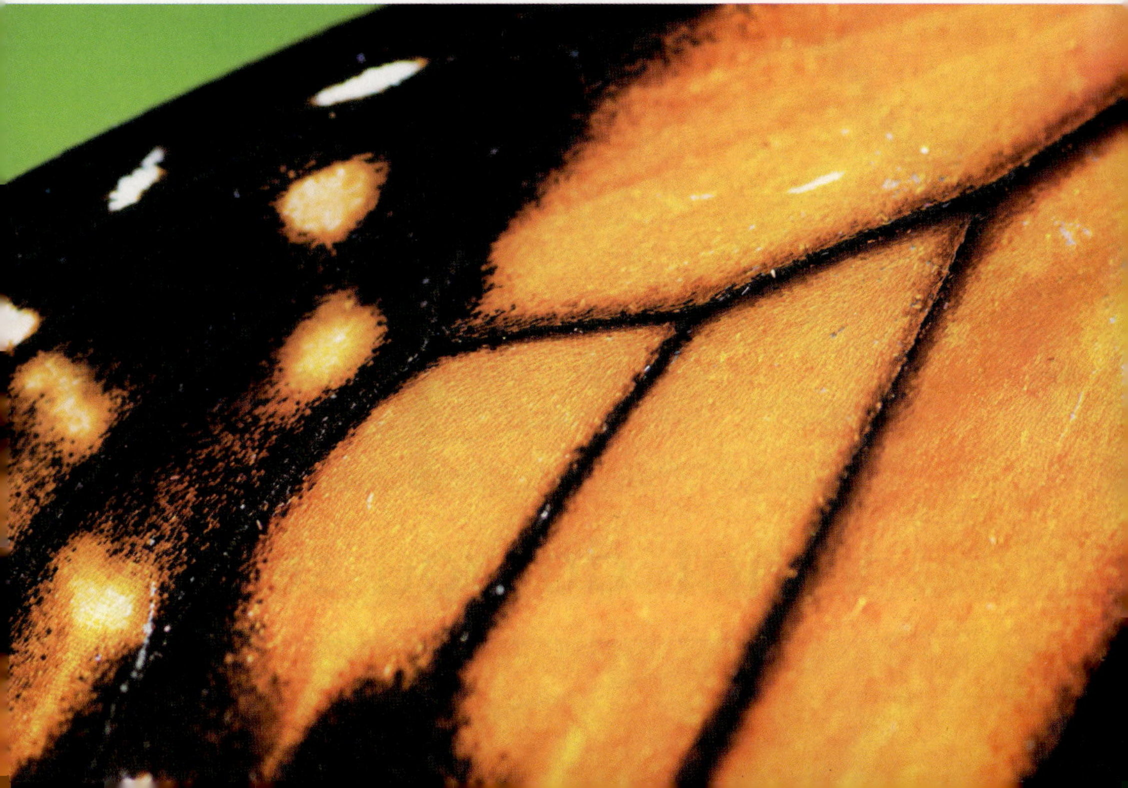

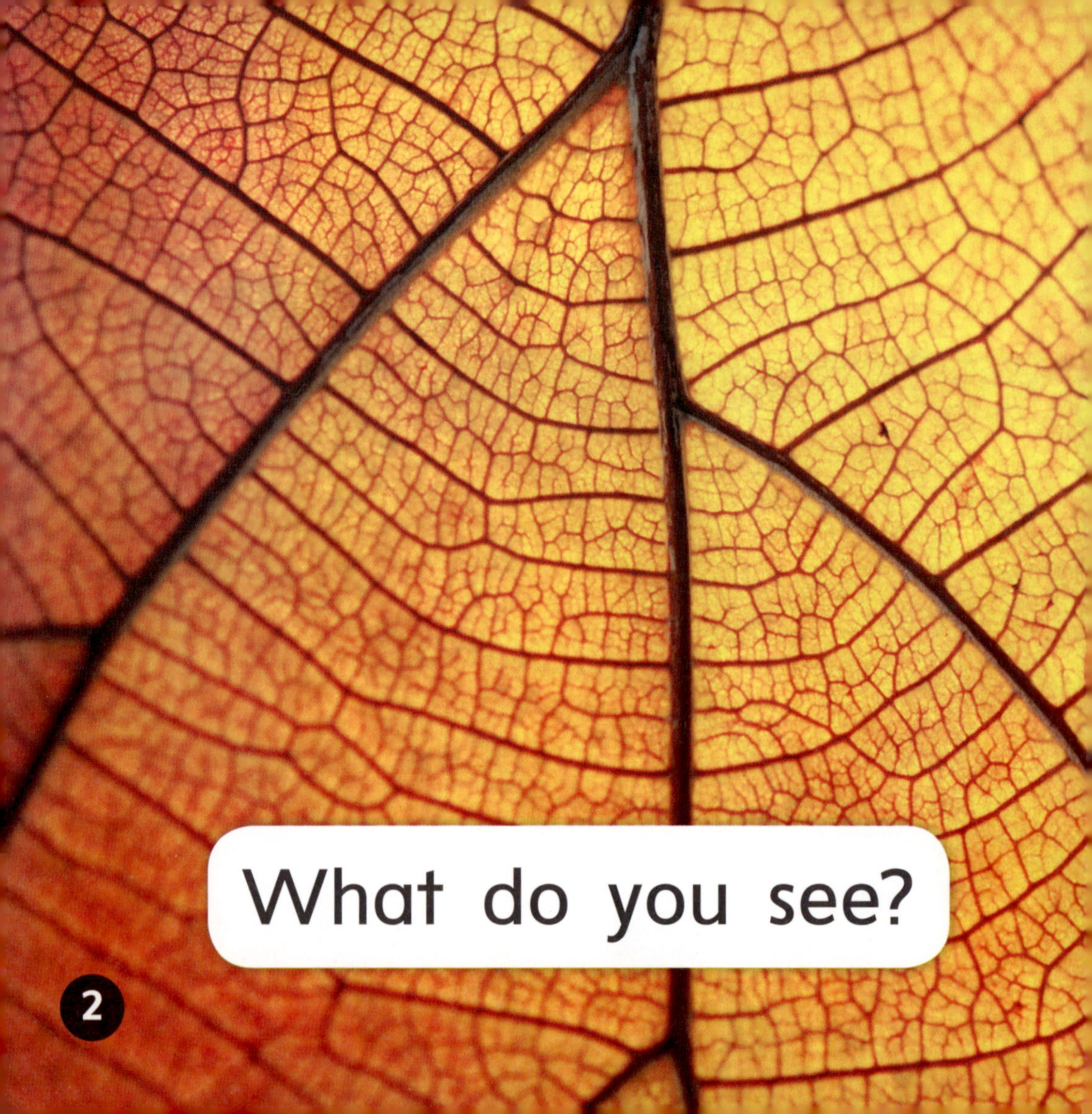

What do you see?

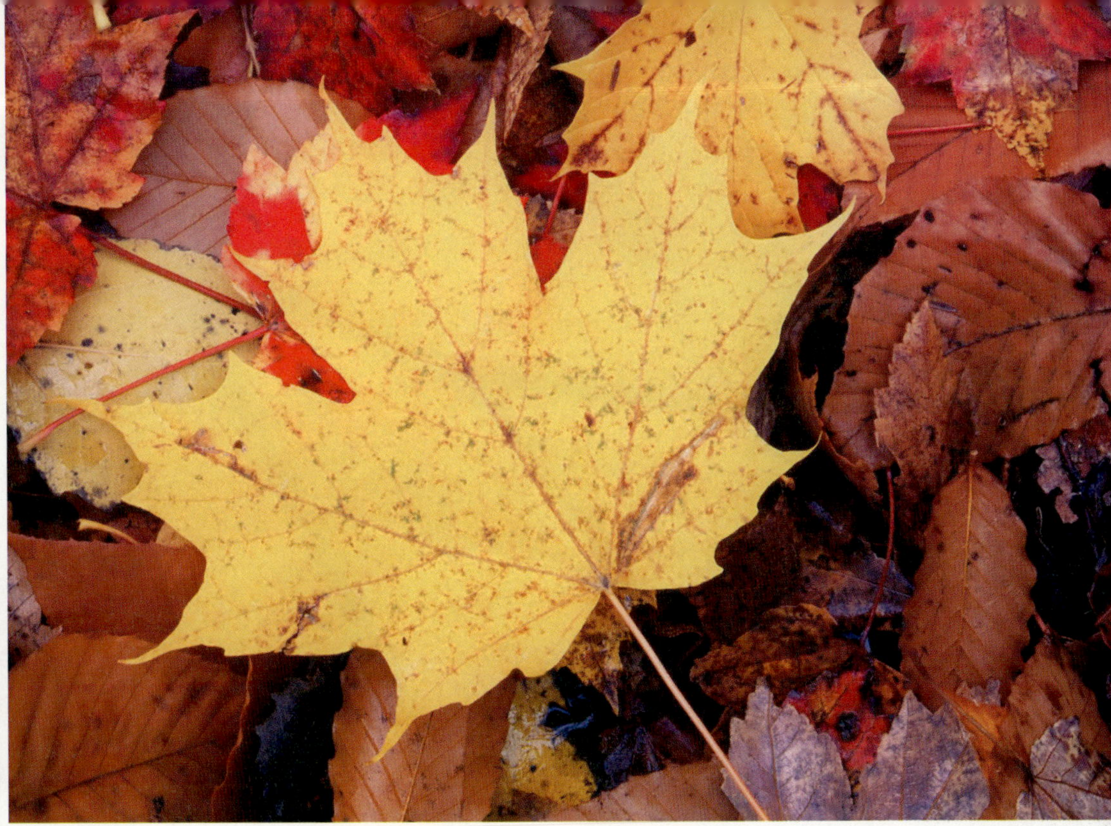

It is a leaf.

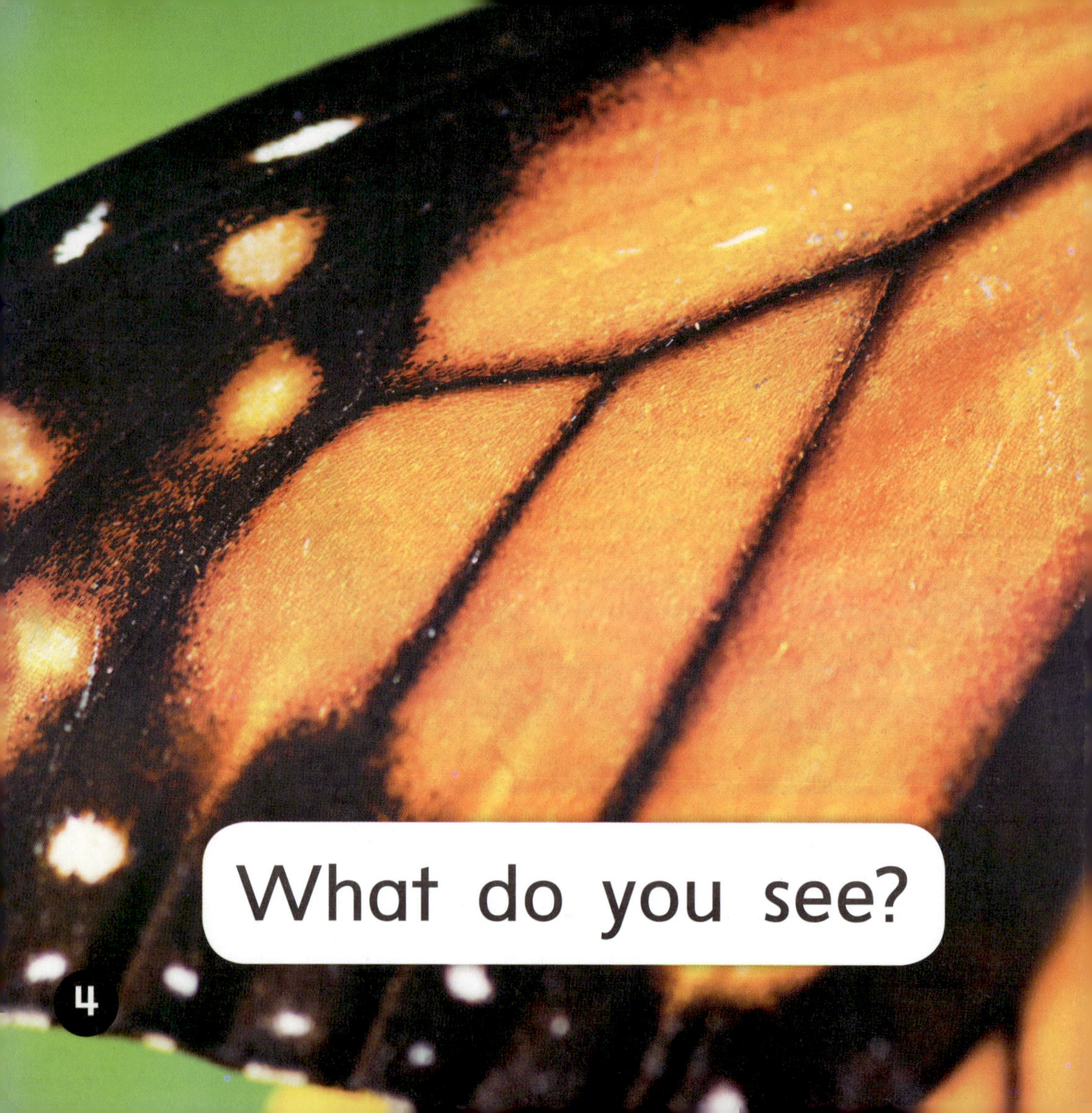

What do you see?

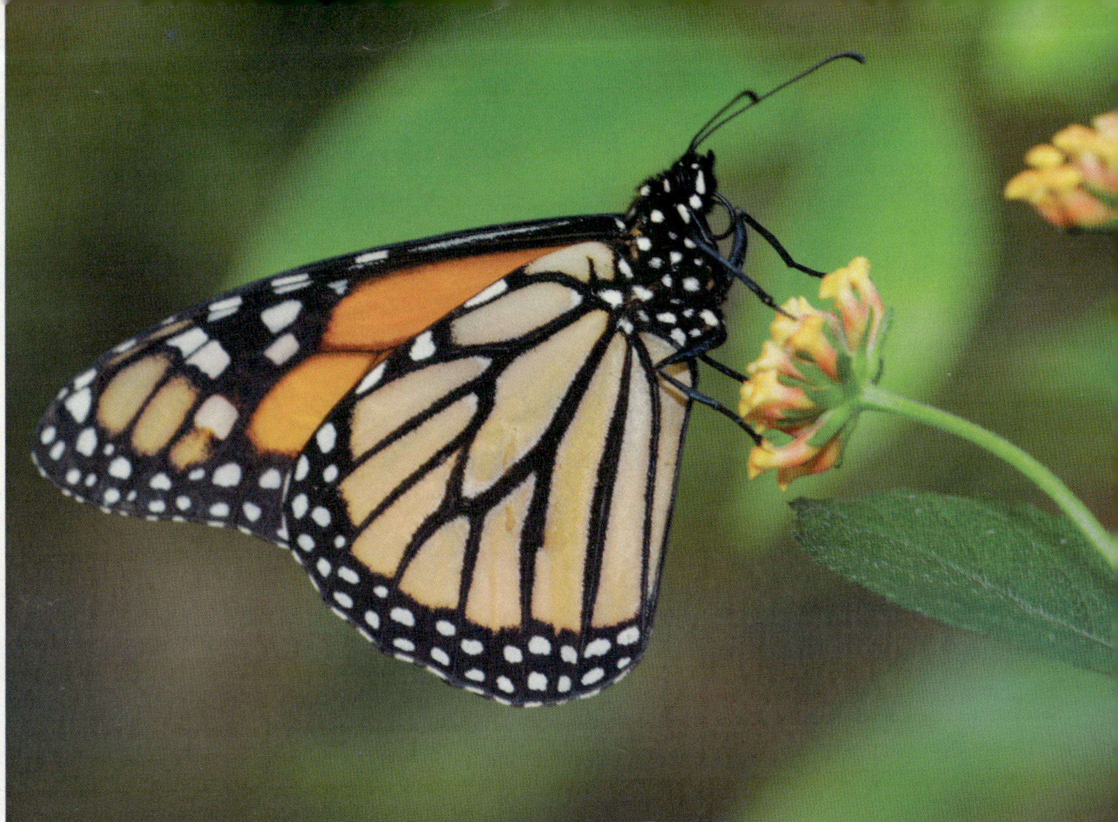

It is a butterfly.

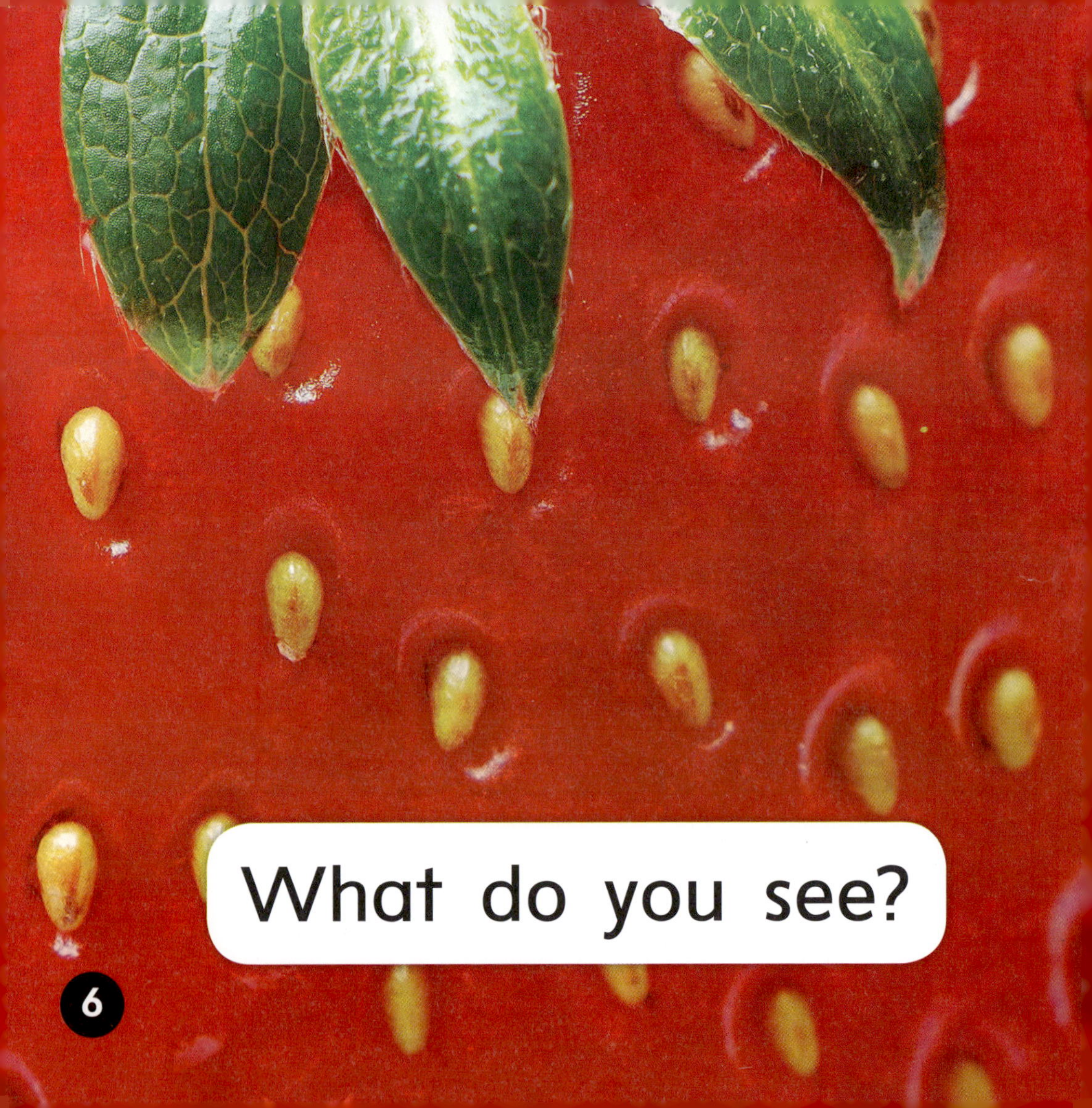

What do you see?

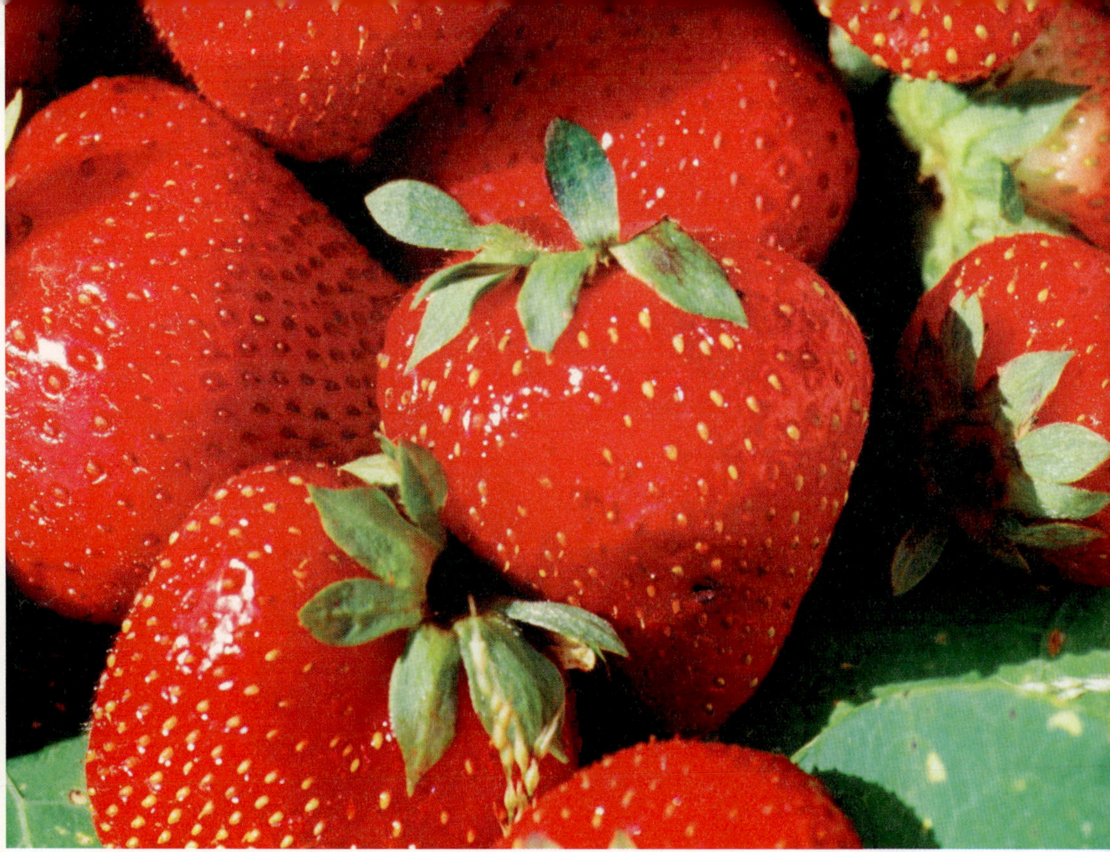

It is a strawberry.

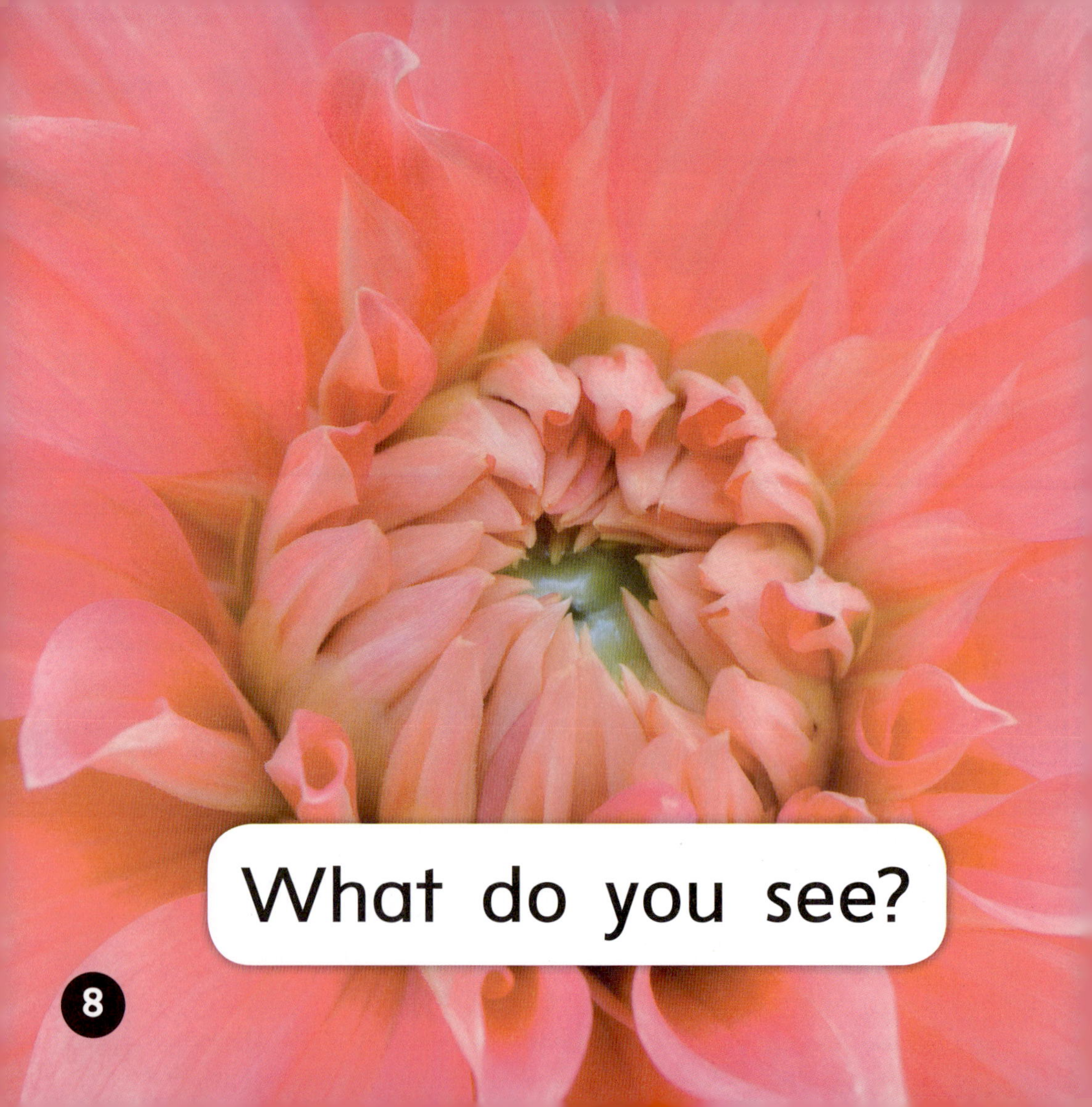

What do you see?